D1637749

GEARED FOR GROWTH BIBLE STUDIES

ABRAHAM

A STUDY OF GENESIS 12-25

BIBLE STUDIES TO IMPACT THE LIVES OF ORDINARY PEOPLE

Christian Focus Publications

The Word Worldwide

Written by Marie Dinnen

For details of our titles visit us on our website
www.christianfocus.com

ISBN 1-85792-887-3

Copyright © WEC International

Published in 2003 by
Christian Focus Publications, Geanies House,
Fearn, Ross-shire, IV20 1TW, Scotland
and
WEC International, Bulstrode, Oxford Road,
Gerrards Cross, Bucks, SL9 8SZ

Cover design by Alister MacInnes

Printed and bound by J W Arrowsmith, Bristol

CONTENTS

QUESTIONS AND NOTES

ANSWER GUIDE

PREFACE

GEARED FOR GROWTH

'Where there's LIFE there's GROWTH: Where there's GROWTH there's LIFE.'

WHY GROW a study group?

Because as we study the Bible and share together we can

- learn to combat loneliness, depression, staleness, frustration, and other problems
- get to understand and love each other
- become responsive to the Holy Spirit's dealing and obedient to God's Word

and that's GROWTH.

How do you GROW a study group?

- Just start by asking a friend to join you and then aim at expanding your group.
- Study the set portions daily (they are brief and easy: no catches).
- Meet once a week to discuss what you find.
- Befriend others, both Christians and non Christians, and work away together

see how it GROWS!

WHEN you GROW ...

This will happen at school, at home, at work, at play, in your youth group, your student fellowship, women's meetings, mid-week meetings, churches and communities,

you'll be REACHING THROUGH TEACHING

INTRODUCTORY STUDY

The Beginning of Everything

The Geared for Growth study The Beginning of Everything: A study in Genesis 1-11 is a good springboard into this study on Abraham's life which covers Genesis 12-25. Here is a compressed history of the early chapters.

Genesis 1-3 gives an account of the creation of the universe, of man, and the origin of sin.

Genesis 4 recounts the first murder, a manifestation of sin.

Genesis 6-8 tells of the multiplication and spread of violence and wickedness and God's judgement on a sin-sick society.

Genesis 9 verses 8, 9 point us to Noah who sought after righteousness and co-operated with God in His plan to give man another chance.

Genesis 10-11 shows the spread of the nations through Noah's progeny and we see, once again, sin and rebellion against God becoming rampant. How will God salvage man from self destruction?

God's plan revealed

To get things into perspective, read and discuss these references:

Romans 1:18	To what is God's character implacably opposed?
Romans 1:24	What does God do with persistent, wilful sinners?
Romans 1:26-32	Do these verses describe today's society?
Romans 3:21-26	How does God get man out of his dilemma?
Romans 5:5-8; 1 John 4:9	How did God manifest His love for us?
Revelation 13:8	When did God's plan of salvation begin?
Genesis 3:14-15	What is God declaring here?
John 19:30; 1 John 3:8	Has this been fulfilled?

'God HATES SIN but LOVES THE SINNER.' Is this statement true?

Righteousness comes through faith

The Bible is full of living illustrations of God working in and through people to accomplish His divine purposes. Some became His mouthpiece to warn of God's holiness and give hope of deliverance from sin. They pointed to a coming Saviour. Others were involved in the unfolding drama of the origin and guidance of God's people, Israel. Abraham is such a man and we will learn valuable lessons as we study his life and character.

What characteristics of Abraham's life are revealed in these Scriptures?

Genesis 12:4	Abraham moved out as the Lord directed
Genesis 13:9	Abraham gave Lot first choice
Genesis 14:11-14	He faced four kings and armies in battle
Genesis 14:18-20	He gave one tenth of his 'income' to Melchisedek
Genesis 18:22-33	He pleaded earnestly for Sodom's deliverance
Hebrews 11:17-19	He put his trust completely in God
Genesis 15:6	Was Abraham made 'righteous' by obedience?
Hebrews 11:6	What is the key to our acceptance by God?

Abraham's background
We can build up a mini picture of Abraham's origins and family from Genesis 11:27-32.

Use the map on page 8 to find the places mentioned, link them with a red line and number them in sequence (in this and ensuing studies) so that you can trace his journeys.

Who was his father? And his brothers?
Where was their home territory? Find it on the map.
What did Abraham's father decide to do?
Who travelled with him?
What significant statement is made about Abraham's wife?
Where did the family settle?
How old was Terah when he died?
How old was Abraham when he moved out of Haran (Gen. 12:4)?

Abraham's home territory
Ur of the Chaldeans is mentioned in Genesis 11:28-31; 15:7; Nehemiah 9:7 and Acts 7:4. Fuller details are given in Old Testament history books, Bible Dictionaries and Commentaries.

We find Ur was located in southern Mesopotamia (now known as Iraq), about 140 miles south-east of Babylon between the rivers Tigris and Euphrates. Babylon, a one time magnificent, prosperous city with beautiful hanging gardens, splendid palaces and temples, fell into gross moral decline. It is the New Testament symbol of opposition to God (Rev. 14:8). Ur also was a prosperous city with well developed educational systems and excellent commerce. Ships traded from the Persian Gulf bringing alabaster, copper ore, ivory, gold and hard woods. As in Babylon, the residents became involved in the worship of many gods and goddesses. Sin, the oon-god, was the principal deity. Ishtar, his wife, was the moon-goddess. he worship of Ishtar deified sex passion and led to licentiousness, 'sacred' ostitution and disgraceful orgies in these heathen temples. Not only were ere prostitute priestesses, but every female, from youth up, had to participate least once in her lifetime in these rites.

Such was the human cesspool from which God uprooted Abraham. God had divine plan for this man's life. In Joshua 24:2, 3 God says:

'Terah lived beyond the River Euphrates
    and worshipped other gods;
but I took Abraham from that land
    and led him throughout Canaan
    and gave him many descendants ...'

od purposed, not only to bless Abraham, but to bless all nations through his escendants. Now we are going to follow God's man through his geographical id spiritual pilgrimages and learn that we, too, can walk 'by faith rather than by ght'.

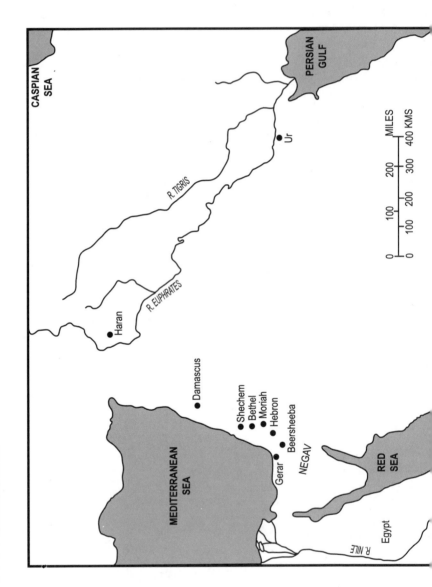

STUDY 1
GOD'S PACT WITH ABRAHAM

QUESTIONS

DAY 1 a) Look up these verses and discuss what you discover about Abraham: 2 Chronicles 20:7; Isaiah 41:8; Romans 4:1-3; Galatians 3:6-9; Acts 7:2,3; Hebrews 7:1,2; James 2:21-23.
b) What do you conclude about this man?

DAY 2 *Genesis 12:1-3. (Look back to the comments on Ur on pages 4 and 5.)*
a) What was God really saying to Abraham?
b) What three things did God promise him?

DAY 3 *Genesis 11:31, 32; 12:4.*
a) Why was Abraham delayed in Haran (Acts 7:2-4)?
b) When did he move on again?

DAY 4 *Genesis 12:5-9.*
a) What could have overwhelmed Abraham at Shechem?
b) How did God deal with this situation?
c) Is there special significance in the altar built at Bethel?

DAY 5 *Genesis 12:10-13.*
a) Why did Abraham head for Egypt, another idolatrous country?
b) What led him to lie about his wife?

DAY 6 *Genesis 12:14-16.*
a) Describe the predicament into which Abraham landed Sarah.
b) Why was Abraham prospered by Pharaoh?

DAY 7 *Genesis 12:17-20.*
a) Who got Abraham out of this awkward corner?
b) What does this teach us about God (Rom. 8:28)?

When God spoke to Abraham His instructions were clear, and in two parts.

1. CALL:	'Leave all! Go to a place I will show you.'
2. PROMISE:	'I will bless you.
	I will make you a great nation.
	I will bless all nations through you.'

Abraham's response is also clear: he obeyed (Heb. 11:8).

Why Abraham?

God singled out Noah because he walked uprightly in a godless society (Gen 7:1). Scripture does not state why God selected Abraham. Did He see in Abraham a longing after the God of Noah? Abraham came of the line of Shem (their lives overlapped) and could well have had a knowledge of God. At a time when this knowledge could have vanished from the earth, God found a response in the heart of Abraham.

'Dragged' or 'Drawn'?

Abraham's first move was made in blind obedience, though he did not do exactly what God had instructed. At times he must have thought: 'I'm mad. Am I following a figment of my imagination?' Pondering what God had told him to do, he could have questioned:

'Me, become a great nation?' (He did not live to see it.)
'Who is this God?' (Abraham did come to know Him intimately.)
'What is the blessing He promises?' (It reaches us today, in Christ.)
'How can I leave my aged father?' (He didn't. He got delayed at Haran till God intervened.)

In the light of Matthew 10:37-39 and Exodus 20:12 we all have to face up to such issues when God calls. Only God can steer us through the maze of circumstances and responsibilities which would deter us from doing His will. 'Haran' can be a divinely planned delay (when we act without seeking His directive) or a man-planned stop (when we haven't totally yielded to that directive). One thing is sure, when we step out in obedience, God does not fail us. The legal 'I must' will eventually be replaced by the 'I cannot resist' which flows from a growing intimacy with the Lord and the knowledge of His ways. Like Abraham, we can be willing candidates in God's school and God is a very patient teacher.

acred Spots

Ve can all look back to special places and times when God specially blessed or evealed Himself more fully to us. At Shechem Abraham may have been surrounded y pagans and pagan shrines (Gen. 12:6). He could have been gripped with fear nd may have questioned, 'From Ur to this?' But God was there. He ensured that Abraham saw and heard Him. The promise was repeated with even greater ssurance: 'I will GIVE this land.' Reassured, Abraham erected his altar of hanksgiving to God. It was the first of many in his pilgrimage. The next one was t Bethel. The altars were a permanent witness to a faithful God. In contrast, Abraham pitched his tent (v. 8), indicating his readiness to move on. His nheritance was ahead. So is ours (Heb. 13:14).

Compromise and Chaos

Famine in Canaan. Plenty in Egypt! Common sense would lead Abraham to a ource of supply. Have a look at Psalm 30:1-3. God had His provision for the sraelites in the desert (Exod. 16:2-8). He would continue to work in Abraham's ife to assure him that He would always provide for him. Egypt wasn't God's way. The way we choose may seem logical and right for us, but God teaches us not to ive by our own wits but by reliance on Him. If we move without the assurance of His directive, we open ourselves to Satan's counterattacks. Fear, not trust, led Abraham into this mess. Only God's intervention (Gen. 12:17) and Abraham's deportation (v. 20) set him on the right way again. He turned back to Canaan, humiliated, laden with provender from a pagan ruler, a sad but wiser man. His attitude had changed when he encountered the King of Sodom later (14:21-24).

Christians aren't perfect, just forgiven'

God's men down the centuries have failed Him. Jonah (Jon. 1:1-3), Samson (Judg. 16), David (2 Sam. 11, 12) and Solomon (1 Kings 11:1-3) were all singled out by God for a specific task, yet failed miserably. God dealt righteously with them and continued to work out His purposes. Failure is never final for the Christian. There is always the way back through contrition and repentance. Yet it is important to remember we are His witnesses (2 Cor. 3:2) and accountable to Him (Luke 12:48). He has made provision for us to know victory in our daily lives (Eph. 6:13; Gal. 5:16-26).

STUDY 2
DECISIONS, DISASTER, DELIVERANCE

QUESTIONS

DAY 1 *Genesis 13:1-4.*
a) Where did Abraham go now? Mark it on the map.
b) What did he do?

DAY 2 *Genesis 13:5-7.*
a) How prosperous were Abraham and Lot?
b) How did prosperity complicate life for them?

DAY 3 *Genesis 13:8-11.*
a) What solution did Abraham have for this problem?
b) Discuss the attitudes of the two men.

DAY 4 *Genesis 13:12-18.*
a) Was God's favour on Abraham's choice?
b) What about Lot?

DAY 5 *Genesis 14:1-12.*
a) To whom were the kings of verse 2 subject?
b) What happened when they rebelled against him?

DAY 6 *Genesis 14:13-16.*
a) How did Abraham become involved in the conflict?
b) What is surprising about his victory over Kedorlaomer?
c) Did Abraham accomplish his objective?

DAY 7 *Genesis 14:17-24.*
a) How did Abraham react to the King of Sodom's offer?
b) How do we know he valued Melchizedek's blessing?

NOTES

By FAITH, not by SIGHT, is God's way for success (2 Cor. 5:7)

Tests of faith, says James 1:2-4, develop perseverance and spiritual maturity. Abraham is learning from his trials. He has had three major ones so far.

Test 1 Exchanging the known for the unknown

At first there was not 100% obedience, and this led to a delay in Haran (Gen. 11:31). Lot was still with him and it seemed his leanings were toward the (seen) things of this world rather than Abraham's (unseen) God. He could be a hindrance to Abraham. Yet, despite these issues, deep down the matter was settled for Abraham. He was going God's way and beginning to grow in faith.

Test 2 Famine

Instead of asking God for help, Abraham used his own wits and landed in a desperate situation. But Egypt (symbol of separation from God) was quickly followed by Bethel (place of communion with God). There he called on the Lord and came into a time of reassurance and blessing. As often happens (Gen. 12:10 and Mark 1:12), blessing is followed by further testing.

Test 3 Separation

The issue of inadequate pasturage pressed Abraham into this decision. The question was: who would choose first? Abraham opted for the unseen (God's still unfulfilled promises) and Lot chose the seen (the rich eastern pasture lands). In short, Abraham yearned for closer fellowship with God, but Lot lusted after wealth and the questionable pleasures of Sodom. Hebrews 11:1 tells us: 'Now faith is being sure of what we hope for and certain of what we do not see.' After the decision was made Abraham viewed the scene from the barren hills, with God, and the promise was renewed (Gen. 13:14-17).

By SIGHT, not by FAITH, is the natural way (Prov. 14:12)

Lot selfishly selected the best. The view eastward delighted him. The lure of the city lights was a great appeal. Abraham was finished with Egypt, but Lot hankered after material things. This would cause his destruction. He headed for the sin-ridden city of Sodom. There is a warning here for us. In Abraham's company there were godly restraints. Lot was benefitting from association with the man of faith. He was coasting on Abraham's faith! Subsequent events prove that the temptations of the world overcame him. The all-important thing in life is to know God intimately through Christ, so that we grow in Him and learn to make God-glorifying choices. This hymn makes the issue clear:

The path that I have trod has brought me nearer God
Though oft it led through sorrow's gates.
Though not the way I'd choose, in my way I would lose
The joy that yet for me awaits.
Submission to the will of Him Who guides me still
Is surety of His love revealed.
My soul shall rise above this world in which I move.
I conquer only when I yield.

Not what I wish to be, or where I wish to go,
For who am I that I should choose my way?
The Lord shall choose for me.
'Tis better far, I know,
To let Him bid me go or stay.

Deliverance

Victory is assured when we are aligned with God's purposes. I'm sure it wasn't easy for Abraham to become disentangled from family. The separation from Lot didn't mean indifference on Abraham's part. As soon as he knew Lot was in trouble he went to his aid. God gave him victory, miraculously, over the enemy, just as he did for Gideon (Judg. 7:14-22). With only 318 men and help from friendly allies (Gen. 14:24) the battle was won and Lot rescued. Right after the victory came another test, to form an alliance with the King of Sodom.

Fortified

But Abraham didn't succumb. He had an encounter with Melchizedek (King of Righteousness) from Salem (City of Peace). Refreshed with bread and wine, blessed by Melchizedek (Gen. 14:19, 20) he exalted God, the bountiful provider (Ps. 65:9). Abraham would not compromise. He had no need for the spoils of Sodom. 'I ... have taken an oath that I will accept nothing ... so that you will never be able to say, "I made Abram rich"' (Gen. 14:22, 23).

Note on Melchizedek:
Halley's Handbook (Oliphants) records (p. 97): 'Hebrew tradition says he was Shem, survivor of the Flood, who was still alive, earth's oldest living man, priest, in the patriarchal age of the whole race. If so, it is a hint that, thus early after the Flood, God chose Jerusalem to be the scene of Human Redemption. Whoever he was, he was a picture and type of Christ' (Ps. 110:4 and Heb. 5, 6, 7).

STUDY 3
GOD UNDERSTANDS OUR STRUGGLES

QUESTIONS

DAY 1 *Genesis 15:1.*
a) Why should Abraham need this reassurance of a protector and provider?
b) Compare Genesis 12:2, 3 and 15:1. Do you see an important factor?

DAY 2 *Genesis 15:2,3.*
a) Abraham's real problem surfaces here. What is it?
b) Under the circumstances who would become Abraham's heir?

DAY 3 *Genesis 15:4-6.*
a) How did God reassure Abraham?
b) How did Abraham respond?
c) What did God do? What can we learn from this (Gal. 3:6-9)?

DAY 4 *Genesis 15:7-21.*
a) How did God reassure Abraham?
b) What did He foretell about his descendants?

DAY 5 *Genesis 16:1-16.*
a) Trace Sarah's actions. Where did she go wrong?
b) What suffering did she bring on herself?

DAY 6 *Genesis 16:1-16.*
a) Assess Abraham's actions and reactions.
b) Why is this lapse in faith so serious?

DAY 7 *Genesis 16:1-16.*
a) List all the negatives and hurts which Hagar suffered.
b) How did God handle her problem?
c) What was her impression of God?

God knows and cares

Sometimes we are not absolutely honest about, or are just blind to, our own needs. We then find it difficult to share the deep concerns of our hearts, but God waits patiently until the real one is expressed. Abraham did have surface fears. He voiced these but just could not see how God's promise of progeny would be fulfilled. It is comforting to know that God always understands (Heb. 4:15), cares deeply (1 Pet. 5:7), and has a plan of unchanging love (1 John 4:10).

He is a 'down to earth' God

He understands the need for assurance and gives His word again (Gen. 15:4, 5). Jesus illustrated spiritual truths from everyday incidents (Matt. 18:3-5; John 4:7-15). God used the stars (Gen. 15:5), the dust (13:16) and the sand (22:17) to describe how Abraham's descendants would proliferate. To back up His word, He pledged Himself in a blood covenant to Abraham (15:9-21). This was another 'visual aid' with which Abraham would be familiar (Jer. 34:18, 19). All this foreshadows the coming of the New Covenant (Jer. 31:31-33; Heb. 9:15) implemented in the coming of the Living Word (John 1:14) and His eternal blood covenant for sinners (Matt. 26:28).

Faith

Abraham 'believed' God. This is the first time the word is used in the Bible. And this faith 'was credited to him as righteousness' (Gen. 15:6, Rom. 4:9-11, Gal. 3:6). What God had promised was good as done for He never breaks His word (Heb. 6:17, 18). When the debits are balanced by credits the account is fully paid. Abraham's faith resulted in God putting over his sin ledger, 'Paid in full'. Whoever responds to God like Abraham did (John 3:16) can be assured that Jesus has paid his sin debt in full. Our faith grows with our deepening understanding of God's faithfulness.

Cultural Pressures

Conformity to cultural pressures which compromise our Christian walk can weaken our faith and cloud our witness. Despite God's encouragements Abraham still had a problem that was bigger than his faith. Sarah was barren and beyond childbearing age. With God's words still ringing in his ears: 'a son coming from your own body' (Gen. 15:4), Abraham succumbed to his wife's suggestion. The cultural solution was to have a child by her maid. How easy! But surrogate motherhood did not solve the problem, and brought heartbreaking consequences. Can we blame Abraham for his impatience? He had waited ten years for the promise to be fulfilled (16:3). The test of time proved too hard for Abraham.

Repercussions

When we act independently of God we bring unhappiness and worse on our own heads. Sarah, Hagar and Abraham all suffered from 'acting God' or trying to help God out in this situation, and the effect of Ishmael's birth is still being felt today.

STUDY 4
GOD SPEAKS, BY SILENCE AND FACE TO FACE

QUESTIONS

DAY 1 *Genesis 16:15-17:1.*
a) How long was it before God spoke directly to Abraham again?
b) How might this silence have affected Abraham?
c) Why do you think God stressed He was 'God Almighty'?

DAY 2 *Genesis 17:1-3.*
a) What was Abraham to do?
b) What would this mean?
c) How did he react?

DAY 3 *Genesis 17:2-8.*
a) What did God say He would do?
b) How significant was the name change?
c) List all the things God promised Abraham. Did they come to pass?

DAY 4 *Genesis 17:9-14.*
a) In Genesis 15:12-18 God pledged Himself to Abraham. Now He outlines Abraham's part of the covenant. What was it?
b) What would happen to any who did not enter into the covenant?

DAY 5 *Genesis 17:15-18.*
a) What about Sarah? How was she to be blessed?
b) In the light of Sarah's actions (Gen. 16:1, 2, 6), what does this tell us about God's character (Jer. 29:11)?

DAY 6 *Genesis 17:17-20.*
a) Do you think Abraham was still having 'faith' struggles?
b) How did God respond to Abraham's heart cry about Ishmael?

DAY 7 *Genesis 17:21-27.*
a) With whom would God establish His covenant?
b) How would you describe Abraham's actions here?

NOTES

Silence

God's silences can be very eloquent! Initially they may cause us doubt and confusion. Yet, as we get to know Him they can only be interpreted in one of two ways.

1. Sin separates! Isaiah 59:2 points out that when we live with unconfessed sin in our lives God cannot hear our prayers and hides His face from us. What is the solution? I John 1:9 shows us the way through. God's instructions are simple and clear. If we confess our sins, God forgives and we walk on in unclouded fellowship.

2. Silence is an excellent teacher. It teaches us to wait on God. It gives us time to review our lives and deal with areas where we have acted independently of God. It shows us what God wants of us. Often that is to rest in Him and wait patiently for His directive. The silence of God in this instance did not come because Abraham had been wilfully disobedient. His heart was set for God, not against Him. He had put himself into a state of confusion because he had acted independently again by not consulting God about the Hagar affair. Was Ishmael God's promised son or not? What God wanted of Abraham was perfect trust. When God eventually did speak, Abraham's heart was prepared to listen.

We are all prone to help God out with His plans. We want to accomplish something for God and surmise we must be doing instead of waiting. Like Abraham, we have to go through God's disciplines to learn that it is the people who know God who will confidently do His work (I Sam. 17:45-47). God says, 'Be still, and know that I am God' (Ps. 46:10).

Walking before God

Abraham was required to believe God (Gen. 15:46). In doing this he was declared righteous. In scriptural terms this is justification. It was just-as-if-he-had-never-sinned.

Now God is bringing attention to the need of sanctification, a life which reveals the character of God. God's instructions in Genesis 17:1 indicate that it is possible to walk apart from Him, with dire consequences (Lev. 26:23, 24).

This is not God's design for His people. Walking is of spiritual significance. Physically, it involves the whole person. It requires faith (in your limbs to hold you up, to move along, etc.). In Matthew 14:28-31 Peter began to sink because he doubted. That is how Abraham 'came unstuck' too. Could God possibly give a son to such an elderly couple? Ishmael was born because of Abraham's lack of faith! Despite God's word: 'I am all you need, Abraham' (Gen. 15:1), Abraham reverted to human conniving. God's message in Genesis 17 is: Walk out your faith! Act as if you expect God to keep His promise! If only Abraham would allow the Lord to fill his 'total vision', all his desires and actions would then be under God's control. This is true for us too. If God is the centre and circumference of our lives then there are no alternatives, just God and His will. The psalmist learned the secret: 'Find rest, O my soul, in God alone; my hope comes from him. He alone is my rock and my salvation; ... I shall not be shaken' (Ps. 62:5, 6).

The lesson God was teaching Abraham is for us too. Walking is not a passive exercise. Our spiritual walk involves: listening (Gen. 17:3-8), praying (v. 18), persevering (in God's Word) (v. 21), and obeying without question (vv. 22-27).

Covenant love

God did not wait till Abraham (or any of us) was perfectly holy before He reached out to him: 'while we were still sinners, Christ died for us' (Rom. 5:8). If we studied all God's covenants, with Noah (Gen. 6:18 and 9:8-17), Moses/Israel (Exod. 6:2-8), David (2 Sam. 7:11-17), the New Covenant (Rom. 11:27 and Heb. 8:8-13), we would see that God takes the initiative irrespective of our sin and alienation from Him.

In Genesis 15 we see God pledging Himself to Abraham. In chapter 17 God is asking Abraham to surrender himself irrevocably and unconditionally to Him.

The seal of this heart allegiance was to be the circumcision of every male. This became the national symbol of the Israel of God. But primarily it was a spiritual sign. It showed identification with God and His Covenant. The outward mark was to be evidence of the inward heart set on God, with resultant obedience (Jer. 4:4, Rom. 2:25-29, Acts 15:5-11, Gal. 5:3-6). It would be hypocritical to go through the rite if there was no intention of obeying from the heart. Abraham's obedience was the key to his 'walking in perfection' before God. God wanted a heart utterly set on Him.

The old covenants established a fellowship between God and His people, but could never give full assurance of remission of sin (Heb. 7:11, 18, 19; 9:1-10). But under the new covenant, through the once-for-all sacrifice of Christ, we can have the assurance of faith (Heb. 10:11-18). We are made perfect in Him (Heb. 10:14).

> 'When you came to Christ
>> He set you free from your evil desires,
>>> Not by a bodily operation of circumcision
>>>> But by a spiritual operation, the baptism of your souls ...
>
> You came ... into a new life
>> Because you trusted the Word of the mighty God
>>> Who raised Christ from the dead'   (Col. 2:11, 12 Living Bible).

STUDY 5

DEEPENING RELATIONSHIPS

QUESTIONS

DAY 1 *Genesis 18:1-2, 16, 20-22; 19:1.*
a) How did Abraham initially see these three visitors?
b) Who really were these three visitors?

DAY 2 *Genesis 18:1-8.*
a) What time of day was it?
b) How did Abraham react to this intrusion?
c) Read Hebrews 13:1-2 and Matthew 25:34-40 and discuss what they say.

DAY 3 *Genesis 18:9-15.*
a) The long 25 year wait is over! What did God announce?
b) Discuss the reactions of both Abraham and Sarah to this news.
c) How did God encourage Sarah's faith (v. 14)?

DAY 4 *Genesis 18:16-19.*
a) Does verse 17 tell you something about the relationship between God and Abraham?
b) How will Abraham become a great nation and a blessing to the nations (vv. 18, 19)?

DAY 5 *Genesis 18:20-24.*
a) What is significant about verse 22?
b) What heart burden did God share with Abraham? How did Abraham react?

DAY 6 *Genesis 18:25-27.*
How are human reason and faith compared and contrasted in verse 25? Discuss.

DAY 7 *Genesis 18:23-33.*
a) Trace the progression of faith in Abraham's pleas.
b) Read Ephesians 1:4-7; 3:20 and Hebrews 4:14-16. On what basis can we have boldness in prayer?

NOTES

Hospitality

What an inconvenient time to call! It was siesta time. Abraham was relaxing near the great trees at Mamre. Sarah preferred the veiled coolness of her tent home. But in true Bedouin fashion Abraham hastened to welcome the three strangers with water to wash hot, tired feet, a place to rest and a most sumptuous meal ('morsel of bread' v. 5 in some translations). We don't know at which point Abraham recognised one of these 'men' as God Himself, but he certainly teaches us a lesson in hospitality (look at Heb. 13:2 and Matt. 25:35). What a privilege to have God visit that humble dwelling! Yet we have Him dwelling by faith in the temple of our bodies (I Cor. 6:19; 2 Cor. 6:16) continually, and sometimes forget Who is in residence!

If Jesus came to your house...

If Jesus came to your house to spend a day or two,
If He came unexpectedly I wonder what you'd do.
No doubt you'd give your nicest room to such an honoured guest
And all the food you'd serve Him would be the very best.
You'd keep on reassuring Him you're glad to have Him there –
That serving Him within your home is joy beyond compare.
But if you saw Him coming, would you meet Him at the door
With arms outstretched in welcome to the heavenly visitor?
Or would you have to change your clothes before you let Him in
And hide some picture magazines – put the Bible where they'd been?
Would you have to turn the Tele off and hope He hadn't heard,
And wish you hadn't uttered that last, loud hasty word?
Would you hide the worldly music book and put some hymn books out?
Would you let Jesus walk right in or would you rush about?

(Author unknown)

Has anyone seen God?

The Old Testament shows He came in different guises to different people. Genesis 16:7-11 describes Him as the 'angel of the LORD' as He talks with Hagar. He was embodied in fire during His encounters with Abraham (Gen. 15:17) and Moses (Exod. 3:2). Isaiah saw Him as a distant figure on a throne (Isa. 6:1, John 12:41). To Joshua He appeared as a man with a drawn sword (Joshua 5:13). In each instance He was heard and recognised, although His glory must have been veiled, at least partially, or the observers would have been blinded, if not consumed, by His holy splendour (Acts 9:3, 4, 7-9). He came to us in the form of a man, Jesus, to reveal Himself as Saviour and Lord. Read I Timothy 3:16 in various versions for clarity.

'No-one has ever seen God, but God the One and Only, who is at the Father's side, has made him known' (John 1:18). Marvel of marvels, we can know Him now, but one day we shall be like Him (I John 3:2) because we shall see Him face to face (I Cor. 13:10-12).

Where are you, Sarah?

In the tent. Overhearing. Thinking negative thoughts. Chuckling to herself in unbelief (Gen. 18:10-12). But where was she, spiritually? Had Abraham failed in encouraging her faith? Had he communicated God's 'promises' of 17:9, 15, 16? God who knows the heart (Acts 15:8), did not condemn her for unbelief. He encouraged her to believe in the God of the impossible (18:14). Nothing is too hard for the Lord. This was God's personal challenge to Sarah to enter into spiritual partnership with Abraham, to know that the promises of God were for her too. The Bible has much to say about the unequal yoke in marriage (Amos 3:3, etc.), but here is a lesson for Christian couples to be truly yoked together as a team for God. I Peter 3:7 touches right on this issue: 'heirs with you ... that nothing will hinder your prayers'.

Where is the family?

The 25 year wait was over. This time the following year Sarah would have that promised son in her arms (Gen. 18:14). But Abraham, remember this: 'It all begins in the home. If you are to become a great nation and a blessing to the world you have to start in the home. Direct your children and household in My ways, the ways of righteousness and justice' (personal précis of verses 18, 19). Read Deuteronomy 6:1-8 and I Timothy 3:4, 5. Parents have a major responsibility to lay solid foundations in their children's lives.

Abraham, friend of God

Abraham was growing in faith and in his knowledge of a faithful God. His life till then had been taken up with personal problem solving. Here we see him at rest about that promised son and at rest in a righteous God (Gen. 18:25). Rest of spirit results from true reliance on the Lord (Matt. 11:29; Heb. 4:3). Abraham was growing to the extent that God now felt He could share His heart burdens with him (Gen. 18:17) and find an immediate response in Abraham's head. The cry for the deliverance of Sodom (for the sake of any righteous in that city – was he thinking of Lot?) was genuine and reminds us of the lesson Jesus taught His disciples on prayer in Luke 11:1-11. ('Shameless badgering' is a modern translation of persistence in v. 8.) Jesus wanted that kind of friendship with His disciples (and with us too!).

'You are my friends if you do what I command. I no longer call you servants ... a servant does not know his master's business ... everything that I learned from my Father I have made known to you ... go and bear fruit ... the Father will give you whatever you ask in my name' (John 15:14-16).

As Abraham pleads for Sodom he prays: in *faith* (v. 25); in *humility* (v. 27); with *boldness* (v. 27).

We, too, can enter into this ministry of intercession with confidence or boldness (Heb. 4:16).

A point to ponder regarding prayer:

'He who has given everything can ask anything.' Jesus earned that right (Gal. 2:20b; I Tim. 2:6; Phil. 2:5-11). We are invested with His authority so we too can pray effectively (John 16:24).

STUDY 6

WE REAP WHAT WE SOW

QUESTIONS

DAY 1 *Genesis 19:1-14; 2 Peter 2:7, 8.*
a) List any good or positive things you discover about Lot.
b) Who were the men to whom he showed hospitality?

DAY 2 *Genesis 19:4-11.*
a) What do we learn about Sodom from these verses?
b) How was Lot delivered from the townspeople's evil desires?

DAY 3 *Genesis 19:12-14.*
a) What did the angels predict? Why?
b) How would you describe the response of Lot's sons-in-law?

DAY 4 *Genesis 19:15-23.*
a) How specific were the angels' instructions?
b) Pick out any major weaknesses in Lot.

DAY 5 *Genesis 19:24-26.*
a) How extensive was the destruction in God's judgement on Sodom?
b) Why was Lot's wife lost?

DAY 6 *Genesis 19:27-29.*
a) What do these verses tell us about Abraham?
b) How did God answer his prayer?

DAY 7 *Genesis 19:30-38.*
a) What was wrong with the daughters' plan?
b) What would later happen to Moab and Ammon (Jer. 48:42; Ezek. 25:1-7)?
c) Where had Lot's choice (Gen. 13:11) led him?

NOTES

Choices! Where are yours taking you?

Read over the relevant notes on Study 2. Lot's choices robbed him of God's full blessing. We should take the events of his life as a solemn warning.

- One wrong choice led to total degradation (Gen. 13:11; 19:30 onwards).
- Identifying with wicked people swamped righteous desires (Gen. 19).
- Lot's choices affected the family for generations (Gen. 19:8, 31-38).

Take a Bible Dictionary and trace the lines of Moab and Ammon. They became a reproach and curse to Israel (Num. 25:1, 2). The one sign that Lot participated in Abraham's posterity was that the Moabitess, Ruth, was brought into God's plan for the fulfilment of His promise (Ruth 1:16, 17; Matt. 1:5).

The Bible is very clear on this issue of choice.

- Choosing wrongly brings God's judgement on our own heads (Isa. 65:12).
- God wants us to choose His way, the way of life (Deut. 30:19).
- Joshua made the right choice (Josh. 24:15).

Read 2 Peter 2:7-10. Lot is here classified as righteous, but his salvation from Sodom illustrates the truth of 1 Corinthians 3:15 and the danger of building on a wrong foundation (1 Cor. 3:11-14). Surely the better way is to walk in Him and His ways and have an abundant welcome into His presence (Matt. 25:21, 34).

God's anger against sin

Read John 3:36, Romans 1:18, 2:8 and Ephesians 5:6. In our Introductory Study we discussed the character of God and agreed that He hates sin but loves the sinner. He does not want anyone to miss out on salvation (2 Pet. 3:9). However, His judgement must come on those who flagrantly, defiantly and persistently defy Him and His holy law (Eph. 5:3-6).

Sodom   'any very wicked place'
Sodomite 'anyone who practises sodomy'
Sodomy   'any unnatural or perverted sexual practice'
                                    (Macquarie Dictionary Definitions)

Throughout the Bible 'Sodom' is used to epitomise evil. If you follow references in the Old Testament you will see the word is used to describe the utmost evil. Our Lord makes references to it in Matthew 10:15; 11:24; Luke 10:12; 17:29.

Revelation's city of sin is Sodom (Rev. 11:8).

This chapter in Genesis shows that solidly, to a man, the total populace was set in evil-doing. Even Lot, though not participating in their way of life, showed he was affected by it in offering his daughters (Gen. 19:8). Ultimately these two daughters were also hardened to sin because of the atmosphere to which they were exposed (vv. 31-36). Sexual perversion led to the downfall of Canaan before Israel possessed the land (Lev. 18:22-25). Paul indicates it was the same in Roman society (Rom. 1:22-32).

Israel, like many of its neighbouring countries, chose to do evil. Pride, sexual perversion, gluttony and prosperous ease were among the detestable deeds in God's sight. No wonder the outcry against Sodom broke the heart of God so that He had to act in judgement on this people. (Mal. 3:1-5)

We live in a day when wrong choices and wrong actions are being made to appear right. But God's Word is clear. Look at 1 Corinthians 6:9,10 and see for yourselves what kind of people will be excluded from the Kingdom of God. There is however, a simple answer for those who want deliverance from the evils of a perverse lifestyle: 1 John 1:9. But the truth of the matter is in John 3:19: those who love their sin reject the light.

Many young people today are being conditioned, through home and school, to make choices based on feelings rather than on the traditional code of right and wrong or on the Bible's teaching. This trend has paved the way to liberty and licence, contravening the Word of God on such issues as sex outside of marriage, divorce on request, drugs, rebellion against parents, etc. It is affecting the whole of society. We need to get back to what the Word of God says and instil it into our children. We need to be praying for God's mercy on, and deliverance from, our godless lifestyle. There needs to be a fresh realisation that we are caught up in a spiritual war. And we need to be assured that righteousness will prevail (Eph. 6:12 and 2 Cor. 10:4, 5).

Intercession

Abraham was burdened for his world. At dawn on the day of Sodom's destruction he was back at the place of prayer (Gen. 19:27). He knew by what he saw that God's judgement had fallen. He would discover later that God had answered his prayer. The one 'righteous' man had been delivered from destruction. His nephew, Lot, was spared. There were not even ten good men to merit God's judgement being withheld (18:32).

STUDY 7

IT TAKES TIME TO MAKE A SAINT

QUESTIONS

DAY 1 *Genesis 20:1, 2, 12, 13; 12:10-13.*
a) Can you think why Abraham should tell this 'white' lie again?
b) What did he jeopardise by repeating this mistake?

DAY 2 *Genesis 20:3-7.*
a) Why and how did Abimelech get out of this dilemma (Ps. 105:14)?
b) How is Abraham described here and what is his duty (1 Sam. 12:23)?

DAY 3 *Genesis 20:7-18; 21:22-34.*
a) How was Abraham's prayer answered in this situation?
b) Discuss Abimelech's character (remember he was not a believer).
c) What ensured that Abraham could live at peace in this region?

DAY 4 *Genesis 21:1-5; Galatians 4:4.*
a) Discuss the issue of 'timing' in God's economy.
b) What good point about Abraham emerges here?

DAY 5 *Genesis 21:6,7.*
a) What difference was there now in Sarah's laughter compared to Genesis 18:12-15?
b) What does Psalm 92:12-15 say about being fruitful?

DAY 6 Genesis 21:8-13; 16:1, 2.
a) Sarah was troubled again. What was her solution?
b) Compare Abraham's response here with the Genesis 16 incident.

DAY 7 *Genesis 21:14-17; 16:6, 7.*
a) Who comforted Hagar in her distress?
b) Read and discuss these references: Psalm 68:5, 6; Isaiah 54:4, 5.

NOTES

Beyond temptation

'The conversion of a soul is the miracle of a minute; the making of a saint is the task of a lifetime' (Quotation from Alan Redpath).

'The best of men are men at best' (Quoted from F. B. Meyer's Daily Readings).

Would Abraham ever get to the place where he was beyond temptation? Can we? James 1:13-15 tells us that temptation can only get a hold on us when the motive of our heart is not right.

Temptation can come to us

- through any of our bodily senses, e.g. lust of the eye (1 John 2:16), gluttony (Phil. 3:19).
- through an uncontrolled thought life (Matt. 9:4; 15:19; Rom. 1:21).
- through giving in to our own desires instead of seeking God's will (1 Pet. 2:11).

Have you got a 'weak' spot, or overconfidence in a 'strong' point, which can pull you down in times of temptation? These people had:

The MAN	The MOTIVE	The RESULT
Abraham	FEAR	endangered Sarah and the promised heir (Gen. 20)
Moses	ANGER	was denied entrance to Canaan (Exod. 2:11,12; Num. 20:8-12)
Israelites	COMPLAINING SPIRIT	robbed themselves of blessing (Exod. 15:24; 16:1-3; Num. 14:22, 23)
Samson	SEXUAL LUST	it brought about his downfall and death (Judg. 14, 16)
Peter	FEAR	was broken with remorse but reinstated by Christ (Matt. 26:75; John 21:15-19)

Temptation is not sin. James tells us it is a testing of our faith and develops perseverance (Jas. 1:3), and overcoming temptation brings blessing (Jas. 1:12).

Giving in to temptation is sin (1 Tim. 6:9). Martin Luther said, 'You cannot stop birds flying over your head, but you can prevent them from nesting in your hair'.

The devil wants us to succumb to temptation (I Thess. 3:5; 2 Cor. II:3).
Christ refused temptation and overcame the tempter (Luke 4:5-8).
He has given us the key to overcoming temptation (Jas. 4:7).

SUBMIT. Put yourself wholly under Christ's control. He understands (Heb. 2:18), is praying for you (Rom. 8:34), and has secured the victory (John 16:33).

RESIST. Don't let the devil get a foothold in any way (Eph. 4:22). Christ came to break his power (I John 3:8). If we refuse him on the authority of Christ we will put him to flight (Jas. 4:7).

Contrasts

Have you ever tossed and turned and worried at night anticipating the worst from a coming event? Then, when at last you face the problem, you find God has answered prayer and things turn out not as badly as you had imagined?

Maybe Abraham's anticipation of possible trouble in Gerar was coloured by what he had seen of Sodom. But he was mistaken. God had brought Abraham to a place of goodwill and peace. Here Isaac would be born. A free rendering of Zephaniah 3:17 is, 'He is silently planning for you in love.' Do you believe that? If you do you will trust Him to undertake in everyday living. (A more literal translation is, 'He will quieten in His love.')

Incompatibility

Faith becomes sight with the birth of Isaac! Abraham is quick to obey the Lord, and Isaac is given the sign of covenant blessing (Gen. 21:4) . But Sarah's joy is marred. For seventeen years she had possibly suffered remorse and jealousy (Gen. 16) and now sees Ishmael as a rival to Isaac. Her attitude seems harsh (21:10) compared with God's graciousness (21:13). The son of the bondwoman cannot partake in the inheritance of the son of the freewoman (born of the will of God, John 1:13b). See Galatians 4:22-24. Ishmael and Isaac will always be at variance (Ps. 83:5, 6; Gal. 4:29). The New Testament teaches clearly that the natural and the spiritual are forever incompatible. No one can inherit the Kingdom of God on his own merits (Eph. 2:9) but those who are saved by grace are heirs according to the promise (Gal. 4:7). Abraham learned this truth at tremendous cost (Gen. 21:11-14).

To those who have found new life in Christ Galatians 5:1 says:

'Freedom is what we have –
    Christ has set us free!
        Stand, then, as free people,
            and do not allow yourselves to become slaves again' (GNB).

STUDY 8

GIVE ME YOUR HEART

QUESTIONS

DAY 1 *Genesis 22 then verses 1 and 2 again.*
a) What did God instruct Abraham to do?
b) Discuss how costly this would be to him.

DAY 2 *Genesis 22:2-4,*
a) Can you think why God would make such a demand?
b) How did Abraham react?

DAY 3 *Genesis 22:5-8; 21:12; Hebrews 11:17-19.*
a) Of what was Abraham utterly convinced?
b) Think of two words to describe Isaac. Of whom does this remind you (Isa. 53:7-10)?

DAY 4 *Genesis 22:9-12.*
a) How complete was Abraham's faith?
b) How did God react to Abraham's response (1 Sam. 16:7)?

DAY 5 *Genesis 22:8, 13, 14.*
a) How was Abraham's faith rewarded?
b) What does the slain ram typify (Lev. 4:14; John 1:29; Heb. 9:22)?

DAY 6 *Genesis 22:15-24.*
a) As the result of Abraham's obedience, what will happen?
b) Why do you think Nahor's family tree is included here?

DAY 7 *Genesis 23.*
a) How many years did Sarah live to enjoy her son?
b) Do you think it significant that Abraham bought a burial place?

NOTES

Tempted or Tested?

Throughout Scripture the devil is exposed as the one who seeks to snare and allure us into actions which will mar our Christian testimony (see Notes on Study 7). He can only make inroads if we let him by becoming careless in our daily walk with God (Matt. 26:41). If he cannot stop us from submitting to the claims of Christ, he will do his best (worst!) to discourage faith, pull us down and rob us of our Christian joy and victory.

The Lord does not tempt us (Jas. 1:13). In order to make us grow spiritually (Jas. 1:2-4) He will test us and try us. The process, like precious metal put through a fire (Mal. 3:3, 4) will sift out the dross of self-centred living. Job puts it this way in chapter 23:10, 'But he knows the way that I take; when he has tested me, I shall come forth as gold.' And Joseph testified, 'You intended to harm me, but God intended it for good ... the saving of many lives' (Gen. 50:20).

Abraham had gone through quite a few refining experiences up to this point, but nothing so severe or heart-searching as this challenge. Would Daniel 5:27 be true of him?

Where is your heart?

Isaac, humanly speaking, could have been the idol of Abraham's life. God's people were later told, 'You must love him with all your heart, soul, and might' (Deut. 6:5, LB). The test at Mt. Moriah would certainly prove who had first place in Abraham's heart. He came through with flying colours! Scripture gives no inkling of hesitation – just utter, implicit obedience. There were only two channels open to him, to obey or disobey. Abraham obeyed God despite what must have been an intense emotional struggle and human heartbreak. His actions declared, 'God first'. Why don't you take a concordance and do a word study on 'heart' right through the Bible? You will find it a heart-searching and soul-stretching experience. Responding to what you discover should bring you to say with the Psalmist: 'All my fountains are in you' (Ps. 87:7). One thing is sure, if you are holding on to an 'Isaac' in your life you are robbing yourself of the fullest joy in your Christian walk.

Faith is substance

This test proved the reality of Abraham's faith. God had promised progeny through Isaac. Abraham knew his God. Even if it meant raising Isaac from the dead, God would keep His promise (Heb. 11.17-19). Do you remember Genesis 15:6? Abraham's faith in God made him righteous before God. Now his actions pleased God (Gen. 22:15-17). Read James 2:17-24. Was James wrong? No, he is really saying, 'Abraham put his faith into action by obeying God.' Jesus Himself taught, 'Not everyone who says to me, "Lord, Lord," will enter the kingdom of heaven, but only he who does the will of my Father' (Matt. 7:21).

Doing is proof of our faith!
Buying the field in Machpelah was a further evidence of Abraham's faith (Gen. 23:16-20). God had also promised land! Abraham would not live to actually possess Canaan, but God would keep that promise and future generations would 'enter in'. So Sarah and others (25:9; 49:31; 50:13) were laid to rest in Machpelah till Canaan was secured. If you need your faith stimulated, read Hebrews 11. Perhaps you have been praying for the salvation of a loved one for years and you haven't seen the answer. The example of these men will encourage you to 'hang in there' and take God's answer by faith. 'Now faith is being sure of what we hope for and certain of what we do not see' (Heb. 11:1).

Spiritual imagery
'The New is in the Old concealed; the Old is in the New revealed.' How true is this statement! Don't you marvel at the Word of God? This 22nd chapter of Genesis demonstrates wonderfully how New Testament truths are held in embryo in the Old Testament. While we cannot let our imagination run riot on 'typology' we can trust the Holy Spirit to mirror in our hearts the unexplained gems in this chapter. Here are a few angles to meditate on; perhaps you have discovered more.

Genesis 22	New Testament Parallel
v. 2 Moriah	Calvary where God sacrificed His son (Luke 23:33)
v. 5 We will come again to you	God raised Jesus from the dead (Acts 2:24)
v. 6 The wood placed on Isaac	Jesus carried His cross (John 19:17)
v. 7 Where is the lamb?	John said, 'Behold the Lamb of God' (John 1:29)
v. 9 Abraham surrenders his son	God gave His only son (John 3:16)
v. 13 The substitute ram	In my place, condemned He stood (1 Pet. 3:18)
vv. 6-9 Father and son relationship	The unity of God and His son (John 10:30)

STUDY 9
MISSION ACCOMPLISHED

QUESTIONS

DAY 1 *Genesis 24:1-7.*
a) What were Abraham's main concerns for Isaac?
b) Which verse shows his faith in God to provide this woman?

DAY 2 *Genesis 24:8-14.*
a) What did the servant promise Abraham?
b) What do verses 12-14 tell us about the servant?

DAY 3 *Genesis 24:15-20.*
a) How did God answer the servant's prayer?
b) How suitable was Rebekah as a prospective bride?

DAY 4 *Genesis 24:21-27.*
a) What was the servant doing in verses 22-24?
b) How did he react to his discoveries?

DAY 5 *Genesis 24:28-32.*
a) What was Rebekah's spontaneous reaction?
b) Discuss how the servant might have felt about Laban's welcome.

DAY 6 *Genesis 24:33-56.*
a) What were the servant's priorities?
b) How thoroughly did he present his master's case?
c) Mission accomplished, what did he want to do?

DAY 7 *Genesis 24:57-67.*
a) How clear was Rebekah herself about the issue?
b) Do you find verse 60 to be an 'echo' of another blessing?
c) On what grounds did Isaac accept Rebekah as his wife?

NOTES

Mission accomplished

Abraham's servant (probably Eliezer of Gen. 15:2) demonstrated that if we rely on God, He will guide us specifically. Look at verses 7b, 14, 18, 19, 24, 27 for example. He totally succeeded in his commission. Did you note the factors which contributed to success?

1. He put prayer at the top of the list (Gen. 24:12-14, 27, 52).
2. He obeyed his master (24:9, 10).
3. He put his master's business before his own desires (24:33).
4. His testimony to his master as a servant of God rang true (24:50).

Verses 27 and 48 hold a vital spiritual lesson for us. The King James version says 'I being in the way, the Lord led me ...' Guidance in crisis decision making came more readily because Eliezer's life style was one of quiet, consistent reliance on God. It was not a hit-and-miss affair! 'The Lord led me straight to my master's relatives.'

If we wait on God like this, trusting Him in everyday living, we will be prepared to trust Him to direct us in making major decisions too.

Learn from Eliezer:

Pray about everything (I Thess. 5:17).
Obey His word (Jas. 1:25).
Seek God's mind and will above all else (I John 2:17).
Let your testimony ring true (I Pet. 3:15).

Building on the basics

Abraham's faith has grown over the years. He is at peace with his God. He is now looking ahead to the further outworking of God's purposes through Isaac. Yet one issue must be settled. He must trust God for the right woman as a wife for his son. Arranged marriages, though a foreign concept to most westerners, are still the pattern in other cultures. In finding a bride Abraham was adamant about two things:

1. Isaac must not marry a Canaanite.
2. He must not gravitate back to a pagan environment.

Scripture teaches clearly that God's children are to marry within the Christian family. See Deuteronomy 7:3, 4; I Kings 11:4: Ezra 9; I Corinthians 7:39 (which surely must apply to initial marriage as well as remarriage after the death of a spouse), 2 Corinthians 6:14-16 (this applies not only to marriage but to every relationship in life). The dire consequences of neglecting God's pattern landed the Israelites in trouble (Neh. 13:25-27).

In this chapter we glimpse something of the eternal purposes of the Father in seeking a bride for His Son. That work of choosing a bride (the church) has continued down the centuries and Revelation 19:7 pictures to us that wonderful day when Christ will claim His prepared bride.

Did you notice in the description of Rebekah's character (Gen. 24:16) that she was a virgin? This is another picture of Christ's bride, kept wholly for Him (2 Cor. 11:2). If Christian marriage is to faintly mirror this pure relationship of Christ and His church, there is no case for today's trial marriages, e.g., 'taste and try before you buy'.

Practical pointers to choosing a partner for life (Gen. 24)

vv. 1-9   *Don't shrug off the advice of Christian parents*
They have proved God, learned from their mistakes, want God's best for their children and desire their happiness.

vv. 10-14   *Saturate the whole issue in prayer*
To pray means to rely on God. The prayer of the righteous is powerful and effective (Jas. 5:16b).

vv. 15-20   *Look beyond natural beauty to quality of character*
Rebekah had good roots. Her beauty was surpassed by her inner qualities (1 Pet. 3:1-4).

vv. 21-27   *Make haste slowly*
All the details were dovetailing but Eliezer was patient in ascertaining if Rebekah was the one of God's choice.

vv. 28-32   *Assess family relationships*
Rebekah had an open relationship with her family, and her parents were discerning and solicitous for her welfare. Family attitudes will carry over into marriage: a young man who loves and respects his mother will usually have the same relationship with his wife.

vv. 33-60   *Determine if there is a mutual spiritual interest*
Rebekah and her family submitted themselves to God's purposes and were obviously sensitive to the will of God.

STUDY 10

LIFE FLOWS ON ...

QUESTIONS

DAY 1 *Genesis 25:1-6.*
a) How many sons did Abraham have by Keturah?
b) Did they share equally with Isaac in his inheritance?

DAY 2 *Genesis 25:7, 8.*
a) Write verse 8 in your own words.
b) List the factors which would have contributed to such a peaceful death.

DAY 3 *Genesis 25:9-11.*
a) What happened at Abraham's funeral?
b) Is verse 11 significant?
c) How much of Canaan did Abraham really own (Gen. 13:14-17)?

DAY 4 *Genesis 25:12-18.*
a) How many grandchildren did Abraham have through Ishmael?
b) What was their attitude to Abraham's covenant line?

DAY 5 *Genesis 25:19-34.*
a) What prediction did God make about Isaac's twin sons?
b) Of what were both Isaac and Rebekah guilty?
c) Where did Esau fail? What about Jacob?

DAY 6 *Genesis 26:1-22.*
a) List the incidents which remind you of Abraham's experiences.
b) What caused Isaac to move from Gerar?

DAY 7 *Genesis 26:23-34.*
a) What happened at Beersheba?
b) Why did Abimelech want to make a treaty with Isaac?

NOTES

Me first!

The narrative surrounding Isaac and his family (Gen. 25:21-34 and onwards) makes startling reading. Partiality, deception, lying, defrauding and carnality are all to the fore. The woman who left home and country to become Isaac's wife is no longer sweet and innocent. Pushed by selfish ambition for her favourite son, she later would deceive her ageing husband, Isaac, indulging his appetite for good food. She favoured the second son and determined to have the patriarchal blessing bestowed on him. Esau was more interested in living it up now than in pursuing a future possession. Jacob, covetous of first place, defrauded Esau and deceived his father. Over all this we could write, 'God has promised – you don't have to scheme' (25:23). Despite everything, God's purposes work out. Follow on with a study on Jacob's life and see how God's grace and patience prevailed. The schemer eventually became the Prince of God (32:22-32).

How do we shape up?

The Word of God points out the possibility of carnal living. Not much further down the line the Israelites were to grumble and hark back to the flesh pots of Egypt (Exod. 16:3; Num. 11:4,5). Jesus Himself warned against living to gratify the flesh instead of seeking Him (John 6:26). Paul teaches that carnal living militates against the things of the Spirit. 'Those who live according to the sinful nature have their minds set on what that nature desires' (Rom. 8:5). 1 John 2:15-17 puts it concisely, 'Do not love the world ... everything in the world – the cravings of sinful man ... comes not from the Father ... The world and its desires pass away, but the man who does the will of God lives for ever.'

We all slip so easily into self-pleasing, self-planning and self-choosing. Thank God for His grace which encourages us to press on, not to live according to our sinful natures but according to His Spirit (Rom. 8:4; 7:21-25).

Abraham's descendants

It is interesting to note the proliferation of Abraham's children through Hagar and Keturah as against those of the covenant line. When Abraham died there were still only Isaac and his two sons in the covenant line! As we trace the history through Jacob the picture changes. He had twelve sons and each of these became a large tribe. Since Jacob's name became Israel (Gen. 32:28) his descendants became known as the Children of Israel. When Abraham went to rescue Lot he could only muster a few hundred men (14:14) but at the time of the Exodus Israel had increased to a nation of about three million (Exod. 12:37). By the time of Christ there were eight million. The Jewish population of the world today numbers around fifteen million (despite the holocaust!).

Are you in the family?

Of far greater significance than the physical progeny is the vast company of those who are Abraham's seed because they belong to Christ and are heirs according to the promise (Galatians 3:29). They, like Abraham, do not seek an earthly inheritance, but are heirs of God through Christ (Gal. 4:7b). Abraham did believe his children would inherit Canaan, but his eyes were on his inheritance in heaven. He was confidently waiting for God to bring him to that strong heavenly city whose designer and builder is God' (Heb. 11:10 LB). No job can substitute for knowing we are God's children and coheirs with Christ in an eternal inheritance (Rom. 8:17). Having the 'birthright' in the patriarchal line carried with it the responsibility of spiritual leadership, the privilege of intimate fellowship with God and the knowledge of being in the line of the coming Messiah. Esau despised his birthright. Later, he longed for it but could not have it (Heb. 12:16, 17). Let us be thankful to the Father who has qualified us to share in the inheritance of the saints (Col. 1:12) which can never perish, spoil or fade, kept in heaven for us (I Pet. 1:4). Abraham, man of faith, lived a full life and entered into that inheritance. The words of this hymn encourage us to do the same:

Chorus: Come on, heaven's children, the city is in sight.
            There will be no sadness on the other side.

            There's a sound on the wind like a victory song,
            Listen now, let it rest on your soul.
            It's a song that I learned from a heavenly King,
            It's the song of a battle royal.
                                        Chorus

            There's a loud shout of victory that leaps from our hearts
            As we wait for our conquering King.
            There's a triumph resounding from dark ages past
            To the victory song we now sing.
                                        Chorus

            There'll be crowns for the conquerors and white robes to wear,
            There will be no more sorrow or pain.
            And the battles of earth shall be lost in the sight
            Of the glorious Lamb that was slain.
                                        Chorus

Now the king of all ages approaches the earth,
He will burst through the gates of the sky.
And all men shall bow down to His beautiful name;
We shall rise with a shout, we shall fly!

ANSWER GUIDE

The following pages contain an Answer Guide. It is recommended that answers to the questions be attempted before turning to this guide. It is only a guide and the answers given should not be treated as exhaustive.

GUIDE TO INTRODUCTORY STUDY

The beginning
If the group has not already studied Genesis chapters 1-11 they should be encouraged to do that study next. Meanwhile, the résumé given in the Introductory Study will give a reasonable background. You can fill in more details as they occur to you in preparation.

If God loves us, why...
People are often puzzled at the sad story of sin, destruction and God's wrath as portrayed in the Old Testament. They do need to understand that a holy God cannot countenance sin, yet, in love, He has provided a way of blessing for sinners.

Co-operation with God
God sought out men who would respond in obedience to Him and become His voice to wayward Israel. The Old Testament story is one long saga of men He moulded and used. Likewise, Jesus' selection and training of the twelve disciples exemplifies His continuing long-suffering patience in preparing 'New Testament' people for His purposes. Today we are still called to loyalty and the 'obedience of faith' so that in and through our lives His love may be revealed.

God changes men
He is the great 'I am'. He cannot describe Himself in human terminology. He says 'I am Myself'. But He is the God of the human race and this means He complements all our deficiencies as we yield to His control. Note the qualities which emerge as

Abraham matures spiritually: obedience, unselfishness, courage, generosity, steadfastness, prayerfulness, faithfulness. Predominantly, Abraham became a man of strong faith. Like Abraham, we may have to start in blind obedience to God's word, but as we prove His faithfulness we will grow increasingly confident in the One who is able to save and keep us from sin (Jude vv. 24-25).

Ur-Babylon
Our world is fast becoming one big urban centre of sophistication, education, wealth (with contrasting poverty!) and pleasure. The righteous God is ignored and people worship the false gods of self-gratification on every level. The New Age Movement is subtly seeking to make Satan a replacement for God, a fact of which we should be increasingly aware and which should drive us further into the Word of the living God. He is still calling people out from a doomed way of life to bless them and make them a blessing to others.

Background reading
You will find a Bible Dictionary helpful in preparing for group discussion. Consult your church librarian or christian book store for reliable commentaries.

Ongoing study in God's unfolding plan for Israel
This study on Abraham may generate interest to proceed with further study on this developing line. If so, introduce the study on Jacob, then Joseph if the group is keen to follow through.

GUIDE TO STUDY 1

DAY 1
a) Abraham became father of the nation Israel. Christ came through his line (Matt. 1 especially v. 17) and through Him came the blessing of eternal salvation. Abraham is known as the friend of God.
b) He is surely one of, if not the most important figure in Bible history.

DAY 2
a) To leave all his pagan associations and follow Him.
b) A land, progeny and blessing (personal and universal).

DAY 3
a) Family responsibilities could have held him there.
b) Abraham was led on from Haran after his father's death.

DAY 4
a) The threat of the ruthless, pagan Canaanites.
b) He appeared to Abraham and renewed His promises.
c) The altar marked a milestone in Abraham's spiritual pilgrimage and would be a silent testimony to the living God.

DAY 5
a) It looked a likely source of supply during a time of famine in Canaan.
b) Fear. See how the devil gains a foothold if we forget God is in control.

DAY 6
a) Sarah became part of Pharaoh's harem and was in danger of violation.
b) Hadn't Abraham given him a beautiful concubine (Pharaoh's interpretation)?

DAY 7
a) The Lord stepped in and restrained the actions of godless men.
b) God is in sovereign control and overrules our human failures in the outworking of His purposes.

GUIDE TO STUDY 2

DAY 1 a) He travelled from Egypt, through the Negev desert to Bethel.
b) He 'called on the name of the Lᴏʀᴅ.'

DAY 2 a) They were both wealthy in silver, gold, herds, tents, etc.
b) Grazing large flocks led to pasturing problems and strife amongst the herdsmen.

DAY 3 a) To split up and each go their separate way.
b) Abraham generously gave Lot first choice; Lot greedily grabbed the best.

DAY 4 a) Yes. Though Abraham moved west to the unwatered hills God assured him of His blessing and continued expansion and provision.
b) Lot went east to the rich plains, but also towards the evil city area.

DAY 5 a) Kedorlaomer. (Point out the battle area to the south-east of the Dead Sea.)
b) They were defeated, Sodom and Gomorrah were plundered and Lot was captured.

DAY 6 a) He heard of Lot's capture and went to his rescue.
b) He fought a victorious king and powerful army with only 318 men. Surely God was on his side (Gen. 14:20).
c) Yes. Lot, his family and possessions were all saved.

DAY 7 a) On account of his promise to God (vv. 22-23) he refused to accept anything from the king (he had learned from his 'Egypt' experience.)
b) As an act of thanksgiving to God he gave back a portion of the spoils of war.

GUIDE TO STUDY 3

DAY 1 a) Abraham probably still had fears of reprisal by the defeated kings, and no doubt wondered how the needs of his household and cattle could be met.
b) God had spoken of what Abraham would receive. Now He declares, 'I the Giver, I am all you need.'

DAY 2 a) He was still without the promised child.
b) The traditional cultural pattern was that his servant would be his heir.

DAY 3 a) He again promised a son and many offspring (Gen. 12:7; 13:15-16).
b) Abraham believed the Lord.
c) His faith was credited as righteousness.
Only faith in God's Word can make us right in God's eyes. Discussion could centre on Galatians 3:6-9 and Ephesians 2:8.

DAY 4 a) He sealed His word with a covenant (see the cultural pattern in Jer. 34:18-20.)
b) They would be slaves in a strange country (Gen. 15:13); they would come out of that country (v. 14); they would come back to Canaan (v. 16).

DAY 5 a) She worked it all out how Abraham could get a son without God's aid.
b) She reaped remorse, bitterness, hatred, jealousy, disrespect and then heaped the blame on Abraham.

DAY 6 a) He listened to Sarah not to God. He tried to wash his hands of the problem.
b) His action brought misery to his wife, heartbreak to Hagar and undoubted remorse on himself.

DAY 7 a) She was 'used', maltreated, rejected, confused, filled with fear and wanted to get out of the situation.
b) He met her personally, told her to return and submit to her master and gave assurances regarding Ishmael's birth, life and descendants.
c) He was a seeing God.

GUIDE TO STUDY 4

DAY 1   a) Thirteen years.

b) He may have thought God had forsaken him because of the 'Ishmael' episode. Or maybe he thought things were all right and Ishmael would become his heir. No doubt he was puzzled and frustrated.

c) God was not only protector and provider (Gen. 15:1) but also Almighty in all the affairs of Abraham's life.

DAY 2   a) Live his life to please God in everything.

b) Putting God in control of every choice and decision.

c) He acknowledged God as Almighty by prostrating himself humbly before Him.

DAY 3   a) Fulfil the covenant made in chapter 15.

b) Abram became Abraham and this was linked to him becoming the father of many nations.

c) Increase of progeny and prosperity. From him would come kings and nations and the covenant would be established. The land (Canaan) would be an eternal possession for him and successive generations.

Yes. All God's word would be fulfilled.

DAY 4   a) Abraham and all his (male) descendants/slaves were to be circumcised.

b) They would not be included in the family of God's people.

DAY 5   a) Sarai (my princess) became Sarah (princess). She was to become the mother of that promised son and the mother of nations and kings.

b) God's purposes and faithfulness are much greater than Sarah's mistakes!

DAY 6   a) He was incredulous! Is he laughing in unbelief or with joy? God is promising a son to a 100 year old man and his 90 year old wife.

b) Ishmael would be blessed, would be the father of twelve rulers, and become a great nation.

DAY 7   a) God's covenant would be with the son of promise, Isaac.

b) Abraham put God's instructions into action promptly and with implicit obedience. Every male of eight days and over was circumcised.

GUIDE TO STUDY 5

DAY 1   a) As three men.
b) The Lord and two angels.

DAY 2   a) Noon. High heat in the East, siesta time.
b) With genuine, generous Bedouin hospitality.
c) Our lives can be enriched through 'ministering' to others.

DAY 3   a) This time next year Sarah will have a son.
b) Abraham, prepared by a previous communication (Gen. 17:16) obviously accepted the pronouncement by faith as there is no comment on his reaction. Sarah revealed her unbelief: by laughing within herself; by musing, 'It can't be; we're too old'; by lying when God questioned her unbelief. (Had Abraham not told her of ch. 17:16?)
c) The Lord assured her that nothing is too hard for Him.

DAY 4   a) There seems to be a deepening bond between them.
b) By teaching his household God's Word and upholding standards of righteousness and justice before the nations.

DAY 5   a) The two men go on. Abraham stays talking with God.
b) His concern over sinful, godless Sodom.
He pleaded for Sodom not to be destroyed.

DAY 6   Human reason says, 'You cannot treat the sinner and the righteous alike.' Faith says, 'You are the righteous Judge. You will deal righteously.'

DAY 7   a) He started cautiously, but made increasingly bolder pleas.
b) Once our hearts are right with God we can confidently plead the cause of others before Him. God is all-powerful to help.

GUIDE TO STUDY 6

DAY 1

a) He was respected in Sodom (v. 1), showed gracious hospitality like Abraham (vv. 2-3), concerned about the evil society around him (2 Pet. 2:7-8), desired to protect the strangers (v. 6), wanted his future sons-in-law to be saved (v. 14).

b) The angels who had appeared to Abraham in Mamre (Gen. 18).

DAY 2

a) The men are singled out as being totally united in godless, sexually immoral living.

b) The intervention of the angels in causing blindness.

DAY 3

a) Sodom was to be utterly destroyed as God's judgement on their sin.

b) As very tragic. They mocked and refused the offer of salvation as people are still prone to do today (2 Chron. 36:16; John 12:48).

DAY 4

a) Very specific: get yourself, your wife and daughters out, hurry, flee to the mountains.

b) A lack of faith in God's ability to protect (vv. 18, 19) caused him to bargain and delay despite the angels' urgent pleading. Was he also still being attracted by the lure of city life (v. 20)?

DAY 5

a) Total: He completely destroyed the cities, their inhabitants, the entire plain and all vegetation.

b) She looked back, that is, she disobeyed the angel's command (v. 17).

DAY 6

a) He went back to the place of intercession, looking for God's answer.

b) The 'Judge of all the earth' had dealt righteously, but had graciously spared spiritually anaemic Lot.

DAY 7

a) Their method of preserving the family line contravened God's law (Lev. 18) and revealed their own degradation.

b) Both would be judged and destroyed by God for sins similar to Sodom.

c) To poverty, loneliness, a cave life, drunkenness and the contempt and disrespect of his daughters.

GUIDE TO STUDY 7

DAY 1
a) Fear overcomes faith again. Sarah is beautiful; he is rich. Any ruthless leader could kill him to get his wife and wealth!
b) Sarah was about to become pregnant with Isaac. She could have become Abimelech's wife!

DAY 2
a) God intervened and opened his eyes to what he had really done. He was to return Sarah to Abraham.
b) As a prophet, with responsibility to pray for Abimelech (I Tim. 2:1-2).

DAY 3
a) God brought healing to the women (Gen. 20:17).
b) He had a healthy regard for God and His servant, Abraham. He was generous (vv. 14, 15) and acted honourably (v. 16).
c) They made a peace treaty (21:22-34).

DAY 4
a) God's timing is always right even when we become impatient (Isa. 30:18).
b) He obeyed implicitly and circumcised Isaac at the right time (17:9-14).

DAY 5
a) The promised child (Isaac= laughter) had come. She could laugh with joy.
b) Believers can rely on the Lord to make them spiritually fruitful even in old age.

DAY 6
a) She resented Ishmael's attitude to Isaac and requested that Abraham send Hagar and Ishmael away.
b) Abraham listened to her, but only acts when God gives His word.

DAY 7
a) As she weeps God sees and answers; she was encouraged by a promise concerning the boy and by the provision of water.
b) God can, will and does prove Himself as the One who is able to meet our every need, if we rely on Him.

GUIDE TO STUDY 8

DAY 1 a) Sacrifice Isaac.
b) He had waited so long for this son. He dearly loved him. God had promised progeny through Isaac (Gen. 21:12). How would Sarah react?

DAY 2 a) If Abraham went through with this, God would know that nothing and no one on earth was dearer to him than the will of God.
b) With prompt and determined obedience.

DAY 3 a) God would keep His word, and even raise Isaac from the dead if need be.
b) Innocent victim. Jesus, when He became our Redeemer.

DAY 4 a) There was no holding back. Despite the human heartbreak he prepared to sacrifice Isaac.
b) He was delighted that Abraham's heart was set on obeying Him.

DAY 5 a) The Lord provided a substitute sacrifice.
b) God's provision for sin, typified in the Old Testament by animal sacrifices which pointed to the Lamb of God, our 'once for all' sacrifice for sin (Rom. 6:10).

DAY 6 a) God's promises will surely be fulfilled. They are repeated yet again (v. 17).
b) Look at chapter 24:4, 29, 58. Abraham did not want a Canaanite 'unbeliever' to marry Isaac. The partner chosen was his brother Nahor's granddaughter, Rebekah.

DAY 7 a) She was 75 when Ishmael was born, 90 when Isaac was born and 127 when she died. Isaac would have been 37 years old.
b) God had promised him all of Canaan yet he had to buy a burial ground! Further evidence of his strong faith (Heb. 11:1)!

GUIDE TO STUDY 9

AY 1
a) That Isaac marry someone from his own family and not a pagan woman. He must also not leave Canaan.
b) Verse 7.

AY 2
a) That he would bring back only a wife from Abraham's family and that he would not take Isaac out of Canaan.
b) He was relying on the Lord to find the 'chosen' one for Isaac.

AY 3
a) To the very last detail, so there was no doubt.
b) Rebekah, in every way, was very suitable: beautiful, a virgin, related to Abraham, respectful, thoughtful, sensitive, diligent, hospitable!

AY 4
a) Evaluating Rebekah and discovering her 'roots'.
b) He thanked God for answered prayer.

AY 5
a) She ran quickly to share these exciting happenings with her family.
b) Laban's attitude would no doubt confirm the 'rightness' of it all.

AY 6
a) He put his master's business before his own comforts (v. 33) and was quick to acknowledge God's sovereign hand in control (v. 52).
b) So clearly and convincingly that Rebekah's family had no doubt or fear about releasing her to this man.
c) His one thought was to return immediately to his master.

AY 7
a) She was willing and instantly ready to go.
b) See God's words to Abraham in Genesis 22:17.
c) On the servant's testimony to God's wonderful guidance and understanding and without even having seen her face! (vv. 65-67).

GENESIS 12-25 • ANSWER GUIDE . . . .

GUIDE TO STUDY 10

DAY 1   a) Six sons.
b) Isaac, as the son of promise, inherited from Abraham, but th
others were given gifts and moved to new territory in N.W. Arabi.

DAY 2   a) See the Amplified Bible for example.
b) Total faith in God's promises, assurance that Isaac would receiv
God's continuing blessing, knowledge that he was going to th
eternal city (Heb. 11:10), etc.

DAY 3   a) The half-brothers were united and discharged their filial dutie:
b) Verse 11 indicates God's continuing presence with Isaac.
c) By faith, all of it (Heb. 11:1-10). Actually, only his burial groun(

DAY 4   a) Twelve, as God had promised.
b) They lived at 'loggerheads' with them (v. 18b).

DAY 5   a) The 'covenant' would be fulfilled through the younger.
b) Favouritism led to conniving and scheming for their own ends
c) Esau preferred to gratify the flesh now rather than look forwar·
to a spiritual inheritance.
Jacob stooped to deception to get what he wanted rather than rel
on God's word (v. 23).

DAY 6   a) Famine (v. 1), attraction of Egypt (v. 2), jeopardised his wife (v
7), incurred Abimelech's disfavour (v. 10), strife with Philistines (v
15).
b) The Philistines resented his prosperity (vv. 16, 22-27),

DAY 7   a) At Beersheba he had a fresh meeting with God (v. 24), the
covenant was renewed (v. 24), he worshipped the Lord (v. 25), an(
made a treaty with Abimelech (v. 28).
b) He could see that the Lord was with Isaac.

THE WORD WORLDWIDE

We first heard of WORD WORLDWIDE over 20 years ago when Marie Dinnen, its founder, shared excitedly about the wonderful way ministry to one needy woman had exploded to touch many lives. It was great to see the Word of God being made central in the lives of thousands of men and women, then to witness the life-changing results of them applying the Word to their circumstances. Over the years the vision for WORD WORLDWIDE has not dimmed in the hearts of those who are involved in this ministry. God is still at work through His Word and in today's self-seeking society, the Word is even more relevant to those who desire true meaning and purpose in life. WORD WORLDWIDE is a ministry of WEC International, an interdenominational missionary society, whose sole purpose is to see Christ known, loved and worshipped by all, particularly those who have yet to hear of His wonderful name. This ministry is a vital part of our work and we warmly recommend the WORD WORLDWIDE 'Geared for Growth' Bible studies to you. We know that as you study His Word you will be enriched in your personal walk with Christ. It is our hope that as you are blessed through these studies, you will find opportunities to help others discover a personal relationship with Jesus. As a mission we would encourage you to work with us to make Christ known to the ends of the earth.

Stewart and Jean Moulds – British Directors, **WEC International**.

full list of over 50 'Geared for Growth' studies can be obtained from:

NGLAND *North East/South*: John and Ann Edwards
5 Louvaine Terrace, Hetton-le-Hole, Tyne & Wear, DH5 9PP
Tel. 0191 5262803 Email: rhysjohn.edwards@virgin.net
North West/Midlands: Anne Jenkins
2 Windermere Road, Carnforth, Lancs., LA5 9AR
Tel. 01524 734797 Email: anne@jenkins.abelgratis.com
West: Pam Riches Tel. 01594 834241

RELAND Steffney Preston
33 Harcourts Hill, Portadown, Craigavon, N. Ireland, BT62 3RE
Tel. 028 3833 7844 Email: sa.preston@talk21.com

COTLAND Margaret Halliday
10 Douglas Drive, Newton Mearns, Glasgow, G77 6HR
Tel. 0141 639 8695 Email: mhalliday@onetel.net.uk

VALES William and Eirian Edwards
Penlan Uchaf, Carmarthen Road, Kidwelly, Carms., SA17 5AF
Tel. 01554 890423 Email: penlanuchaf@fwi.co.uk

JK CO-ORDINATOR
Anne Jenkins
2 Windermere Road, Carnforth, Lancs., LA5 9AR
Tel. 01524 734797 Email: anne@jenkins.abelgratis.com

UK Website: www.wordworldwide.org.uk

Christian Focus Publications

publishes books for all ages

Our mission statement –

STAYING FAITHFUL

In dependence upon God we seek to help make His infallible word, the Bible, relevant
Our aim is to ensure that the Lord Jesus Christ is presented as the only hope to
obtain forgiveness of sin, live a useful life and look forward to heaven with Him.

REACHING OUT

Christ's last command requires us to reach out to our world with His gospel. We
seek to help fulfill that by publishing books that point people towards Jesus and
help them develop a Christ-like maturity. We aim to equip all levels of readers for
life, work, ministry and mission.

Books in our adult range are published in three imprints.

Christian Focus contains popular works including biographies, commentaries,
basic doctrine, and Christian living. Our children's books are also published in
this imprint.

Mentor focuses on books written at a level suitable for Bible College and seminary
students, pastors, and other serious readers; the imprint includes commentaries,
doctrinal studies, examination of current issues, and church history.

Christian Heritage contains classic writings from the past.